FAITH:

SILENT STRENGTH

(AN ANTHOLOGY OF POEMS)
(PAPERBACK, NOVEMBER 2024)

COMPILED & EDITED BY
DR. SONIA GUPTA

NOVEMBER 2024

SELF-PUBLISHED
At
Notion Press

DEDICATED TO

Walk by
FAITH
not by sight

CONTENTS

FOREWORD

About the Faith That Governs Life

In our life paths we encounter difficulties, suffering, dark clouds. Beyond the hopelessness, however, there is a glimmer of hope. Magical music lifts us up. Day and night change, winter and summer turn, we can ever though reach the wreath of success, working for it.

*Believing in her powers and the talent of the poets included in this collection, Dr. Sonia Gupta presents a new book, this time dedicated to FAITH. After more than the dozens of successful anthologies related to the most essential themes in life: love, friendship, fatherhood, motherhood, determination, smile, music, passion, miracles, gratitude...etc, for which I had the honor of writing forewords or reviews, here is the new pearl of the series, "**FAITH: SILENT STRENGTH",** ".*

The volume seems to be designed to fill us with optimism, to make us believe in the significance of our existence. Poets convince us that we will win the race, dreams will carry us forward. Belief in one's abilities is the most powerful driving force. We encounter a lot of pain and sadness around us every day. We are advised to overcome the darkness, to think beyond negativity, to tame the heart with patience, not to lose our confidence, to plant and tend the tree of faith and to never allow the thought of defeat and loss, to keep our head high. Faith is a deep and unceasing trust in God. It brings us hope. Man can disappoint us, the Most High - never. People who doubt are like waves of the sea, tossed by the winds. Faith displaces fear, keeps our inner fervor and enthusiasm alive. With their calligraphy, poets paint pictures of light for the future.

The creator of the impressive anthology is Dr. Sonia Gupta - known as an author, reviewer, editor, translator, artist and doctor by profession. She compiled with skill and expertise over dozens of anthologies on various subjects for which I had the honour of writing forewords or reviews. They have made a high contribution to the development of poetry and brought excitement, joy, many emotions and wisdom to their many readers around the world on their fine pages. The present volume is another beautiful bird that flies to the readers. Today again it is my pleasure to write the foreword for her new anthology. Her monthly published literary e-magazine, 'Canvas of Thoughts', each issue of which is dedicated to a different theme, has gained wide popularity. Admirations to Dr. Sonia Gupta for her tireless efforts to take the art of poetry to greater heights. Our congratulations and gratitude to the literary devotee Dr. Sonia Gupta as well as to the talent and positivity of the poets included in this remarkable anthology, designed to raise the level of readers and increase confidence in the rightness of the chosen path, of faith in humanity. I am sure, this anthology will leave a positive mark on the pages of literature forever.

Stoianka Boianova
(Poet, Reviewer & Critic)
Sofia, Bulgaria

A Journey Through the Worlds

I felt immortal when I was a little girl -
I believed that no one could harm me,
My relatives took care of me,
The starry sky protected me -
I came out of my body in dreams,
When I was attacked by enemies.

I became insecure over the years,
I was wondering how to live in these houses,
Which anyone can sell them,
The fate had sent me,
Among sand towers,
I believe in the Higher Idea –

I was on a harmonious planet,
With heavenly landscapes,
I'm here today,
This world is mine too,
God redirects my soul,
On her way through the worlds.

About the Reviewer

She is a poet, writer, author, editor and reviewer. She has authored eleven books: poetry, novel and short stories. and co-authored four bilingual books, poetry and haiku – in India with Minko Tanev. She has participated in over 60 international anthologies and publications with numerous awards and recognitions. She edits dictionaries and books. She is in the European Top 100 of the most creative haiku authors. She won several awards, "First World Poetry Competition of Newspapers and Televisions", 2020, China, Chinese International Zhengxin Poet Award, 2022, International Poetry Prize "Ossi di Seppia", 2023, Italy. She is a Chairwoman of Haiku Club – Plovdiv, an editorial board member of "Haiku Sviat/Haiku World" magazine. She is also a member of PEN Bulgaria, Union of the Bulgarian Writers, the Bulgarian haiku Union, the Haiku Foundation – USA, United Haiku and Tanka Society – UK, the World Haiku Association, Japan, Global Honorary Council of Federation of World Culture & Art Society (Singapore). She is a Physicist and has worked in the field of measurement accuracy - metrology, standardization, certification, authorization.

- ***Facebook ID***: *https://www.facebook.com/stoianka.boianova.3*
- ***Email ID***: *stboianova@abv.bg*

PREVIEW-1

Faith is the Silent Strength That Brings Patience and Tolerance

*Faith makes us rise above the material world, to understand that there is another reality - that of God, the creator of everything visible and invisible. Here are some of the questions we become empathetic to with the new anthology **"FAITH: SILENT STRENGTH"** compiled & edited by the famous name Dr. Sonia Gupta, established as an author and editor with multiple poetry collections. The selected verses teach us that with faith and positivity, we would cross the spaces beyond darkness and negativity, we would sow and nurture the seeds of spirituality. We would water the new sprouts of knowledge and wisdom reflected in these works, and give them access to the light and air they crave. The spiritual fruits of future humanity would delight us. Poets' appeals to preserve our hope are touching. People can let us down, but our God never. His insights are true, His language is that of love. The believers - there is no doubt in their minds. God's words are not ambiguous, they are always clear. Those consecrated in all His future plans will be exalted. Their deep trust in God's power makes them live in harmony. When life pushes us into a corner and we seem to have no way out, some may cower in fear, and others may scream in despair. The authors suggest us to preserve dignity even in misfortune. Our unshakable conviction will attract positive energies. It is an option to find strength to overcome difficult situations. There is hope in the poems - in every darkness, there is a light, and for every pain, there can be healing. It gives us the courage to believe: truth triumphs and shines. Faith brings patience and tolerance, keeping it is the key to opening the door of expectation. It leads us to a life filled with blessings.*

Dr. Sonia Gupta is an established poet and author of twenty-five independent books, editor of several anthologies, poems and magazines, translator and reviewer. I feel glad to be a part of her projects. Presenting anthologies on meaningful and important themes, she is doing a remarkable job in the field of literature that will be admired forever. Today, again it's my pleasure to scribble my words for her new anthology, ***"FAITH: SILENT STRENGTH"****. We are grateful to Dr. Sonia Gupta and the poets for inspiring optimism. Indeed it is a beautiful compilation that invites us to give in to the urge, to live with self-belief and optimism in every phase of life. Faith is the silent strength that brings patience and tolerance, keeping it is the key to opening the door of expectation. It leads us to a life filled with blessings. My congratulations to Dr. Sonia Gupta and all the poets for their determined spirit to create this new anthology.*

- Minko Tanev
(Poet, Reviewer & Critic)
Sofia, Bulgaria

My Belief

White thorns
With donkey thistles
Are knitting thorn wreath -
New Testament symbol
Of the suffering.

Parody crown of thorns
To atone for our sin -
Has cried out a haughty sneer
Over the millennia.

Ellipses shape inflorescences bloom
Pink or dark red -
Analog of shed blood
With the Son of God on the cross
And the Ascension
Bless us
Heavenly enlightenment.

© ***Minko Tanev***

About the Reviewer

He is a poet, writer, author, editor and reviewer. He has authored 6 books and co-authored 4 bilingual books, poetry and haiku – in India with Stoianka Boianova. He has participated in over 60 International anthologies and publications with numerous awards and recognitions. He has edited over 70 books. He is in the European Top 100 of the most creative haiku authors. He has won several awards, "First World Poetry Competition of Newspapers and Televisions", 2020, China, Chinese International Zhengxin Poet Award, 2022, International Poetry Prize "Ossi di Seppia", 2023, Italy. He is a member of Union of the Bulgarian Writers, the Bulgarian haiku Union, the Haiku Foundation – USA, United Haiku and Tanka Society – UK, the World Haiku Association, Japan, Global Honorary Council of Federation of World Culture & Art Society (Singapore). He is a Philologist - Bulgarian language. He was a lecturer of Bulgarian language for foreign students – Medical University, Plovdiv.

Facebook ID: *https://www.facebook.com/minko.tanev.9*
Email ID: *minkotanev@abv.bv*

PREVIEW-2

"Faith is taking the first step even when you don't see the whole staircase"

- Martin Luther King Jr.

Very well expressed in the above quote about the value of a small word known as 'Faith'. When we cross the hurdles and obstacles of life's pathway, and we don't understand where to move, at that time our Faith becomes the first step that we take without knowing the final destination. Faith is a magical power that can bring miracles turning impossibilities into possibilities and hurdles themselves move away looking at the powerful impact of Faith. And it is absolutely true, amidst crisis and odds, Faith serves as the greatest silent strength.

Taking "Faith" as the central theme of this anthology, renowned editor Dr Sonia Gupta has again come up with a new collection of poems ***"FAITH: SILENT STRENGTH".*** *This anthology consists of fifty poems composed by fifty poets from different parts of the world, in which each poet offers a unique and beautiful outlook on faith and what it means to them. Their words speak of strong conviction of faith, hope and the courage to keep on believing no matter what hurdles life puts in your way. That faith can keep you strong and resilient, even when there is no one else to turn to, no one else around, when you are all that you have. Thus these verses justify the title of book too.*

Dr. Sonia Gupta has already edited numerous anthologies and write-ups of different poets and authors throughout the world. This current anthology ***"FAITH: SILENT STRENGTH"****. is yet another achievement for her as an Editor. A renowned author of*

25 independently published books in English and Hindi, she is making her mark on the pages of literature with her contributions. I am very honoured to be a part of her projects, for which I wrote previews. This for me has been and will continue to be very memorable. I am truly amazed by the way she accomplishes her tasks before the given time. Presenting different poets from different regions on a single platform and providing them with the opportunity to contribute to literature altogether is an appreciable effort made by her. I congratulate her on yet another wonderful anthology that is enriched with powerful impacts of this small word known as 'FAITH', turning impossible into possible, leading to the way of success and blessings.

-Donna McCabe

(Poet & Reviewer)

Rhondda, South Wales, UK.

Mortals Lost Glory

We are but mere mortals
Upon this planet, we call Earth
Yet finding glory in god's above
Giving thanks for joy and rebirth
Yet we forget that we can
Find glory here too
In the life, we are living right now
By living life to the full
And achieving our long-held goals
We can ascend into the next life
With a pure and hearty soul
So let's make the most
Of this life right now
Plough on and love the life we're in
Count our blessings every day
Just enjoy being a mere mortal
Just avoiding sin.

© ***Donna McCabe***

About the Reviewer

She is an established poet with over 20 years of experience whose vast variety of work has gained her multiple accolades within her field of literature over the years. From being published in journals, magazines and anthologies as well as being a highly respected admin in multiple social media groups, she is a regular contributor to literature. Besides this, she is an artist also. Her intricate wordplay displayed in her works has been personified by her past and concurrent experiences which include her hardships, trials and tribulations. Her lifetime admiration of reading and writing and love of art has steered her into an adventurous new direction of collaborations with an up-and-coming Canadian artist Ala Ilescu whose idiosyncratic mind and artistic works compliment the vivid images her narrative works paint. These collaborations have resulted in a beautiful book of poetry and artwork entitled "Explosion of Love" published on Amazon. Her creativity has also taken her onto other platforms in recent times, Using Instagram to reach out and display her love of writing, artwork, and love of the natural world to a wider audience. Her writings and interactions with the wider poetry communities there have helped her gain a good following and many features and awards.

- ***Email id-*** *donna_salisbury@sky.com*
- ***Instagram page*** *-@donnamccabe_*
- ***Facebook page-*** *Poemsbydonnamcc*

PREFACE

Life is uncertain, full of hurdles and odds. At every step, there is a new obstacle. And in all relationships, multiple conflicts exist, knitting a cobweb of issues. In those tough and delicate times, there is one biggest strength within us which helps us to adapt ourselves in those situations and mould us accordingly in a positive way. And that strength is nothing but our belief/ FAITH. Without FAITH, no relation can be formed, and no bonding can be created. Without FAITH, we can never reach our destination. FAITH is the first step toward any journey. If we keep FAITH in ourselves and God, life itself opens the pathways to success.

We have published several anthologies on different themes to date. Continuing that journey, a thought came into my mind to bring a new anthology dedicated to FAITH. And the current anthology ***"FAITH: SILENT STRENGTH",*** *in your hands is the result of that thought. It is a compilation of 50 poems composed by 50 poets from around the globe. Through these poems, poets have expressed their different thoughts towards this virtue known as 'FAITH'. For some, FAITH is their inspiration; for others, it is their companion; for others, it is their vision for tomorrow. Overall, all verses signify the value of keeping FAITH in oneself; FAITH is the biggest strength that can fight any adverse situation silently. Contributions by many budding young poets have added more beauty to this anthology. These poetic souls are the inspiration for other poets and writers.*

As an Editor, I had a huge responsibility on my shoulders to select the poems, compile, edit and design this anthology. I have tried my best to accomplish my job. Here, one thing I would like to highlight is that the role of editing regarding punctuation, commas, capitalization of the first letter, etc. is excluded from my side because different poets had their own assumptions and not everyone was happy to follow a common rule. So, the poems have been placed as per the choice of the poets. For any plagiarism, the editor is not responsible, poets have submitted their poems along with a declaration. The entire anthology has been designed by me, including the cover page. The picture on the cover page has been taken from internet resources. Though I am an artist and wanted to paint it myself, owing to some health issues, it was not possible this time. I appreciate the timeless contribution, dedication, and cooperation shown by the poets from day one until the end of this project. I am sure after reading these verses, everyone will start believing in their own potential and feel the magic of this simple virtue that leads to crossing all odds and hurdles coming on life's pathway. I congratulate my entire team, including the poets and reviewers for their wonderful contributions. Let us keep alive this flicker of FAITH to attain a blissful and prosperous tomorrow.

- Dr. Sonia Gupta
(Editor)

ACKNOWLEDGEMENTS

I usually hear these words: "If we say Thank You to someone, it means we are bowing our heads in front of that Lord only". We can forget anything in life, but we should never forget to Thank someone who has helped or motivated us in any way. I am a medical professional and I never thought that one day I would become a writer, poet and author. It is all a miracle and a dream for me. But now it has become my passion, my inspiration and an integral part of my life. It's all by God's grace that he honoured me with such a unique gift. And the amazing aspect of this achievement is that everything I have gained during the odd and dark phase of my life. To accomplish any task, there are many invisible hands behind which shower abundant blessings, motivating us to achieve our destination. In the same way, in completing this book, I have been blessed and encouraged by so many for whom I am GRATEFUL by my heart.

First of all, I thank the Goddess of knowledge and wisdom, Maa Saraswati, who gave me the strength to complete this work and encouraged me to pick up my pen to compile, edit and prepare this anthology. In the world, everything changes, but one thing that never changes is our parents. Heartfelt thanks to my parents for their faith in me and showering their infinite blessings on me. Special thanks to my father, who has left this materialistic world to attain the embrace of the divine Lord. He had been my inspiration and will be forever, and his teachings illuminate my life's pathway like an enlightening candle. Thank you Mom, for being there throughout my work and for all your support and blessings.

A huge bundle of thanks to all the authors and poets, who have put in their endless efforts by contributing their wonderful poems that represent the theme of this anthology. Most of the poets are much more senior than I am, and I pay my respect and honour to all of them for their full cooperation from day one of this project until the very last moment, respecting my guidelines.

A token of thanks to the poet ***'Stoianka Boianova'*** *from Bulgaria for writing a wonderful foreword for this anthology. Thank you for all your blessings and support. My gratitude goes out to the international poets* ***'Minko Tanev'*** *from Bulgaria &* ***'Donna McCabe'*** *from the UK for taking out their valuable time to write the previews for this anthology despite their busy schedules. Thank you both of you, your words have beautified our anthology.*

A word of thanks to all my respected teachers who always showed me the right path in my life and brimmed my heart with their blessings. A lovable token of gratitude to my brothers, sisters and all family members for their love and support always. My regards and love to all friends, far and near. Special thanks to all children of the world to whom we have dedicated this anthology. Last but not least, it will be unfair if I forget to thank the Notion Press publishers, through whom the publication of this book has become possible. Thanks to the entire team for the cooperation. Thank you, readers, fellow poets and friends, for all your love and appreciation.

Thank you!

Dr. Sonia Gupta
(Edito

MEET THE EDITOR

Dr. Sonia Gupta (Dera Bassi, Mohali, Punjab, India)

Dr. Sonia Gupta is a poet, writer, author, reviewer, editor and translator. She writes in English, Hindi, and Punjabi languages. By profession, she is a Dentist (MDS) with a major specialisation in Oral and Maxillofacial Pathology. She writes in vivid genres of literature like poetry, stories, essays, letters, songs and many more. She has established herself as a renowned author after getting her 25 solo books published to date, of which 11 are in English and 14 are in Hindi. Her English books are poetic collections entitled 'Spectrum of Life', 'Canvas of Life...with My Pen', 'Fountain of Inspirations', 'Meeting My Soulmate', 'Silent Verses', 'Mysterious Musings of Life', 'Agony of Life', 'Miracle of Virtues', 'Acrostic Motivations', 'There is No Darkness' and 'In the Embrace of Love'. Her first English novel is coming soon. Her Hindi books include 13 collections of poetry entitled 'Zindagi Gulzar Hai', 'Ummid Ka Diya', 'Kabhi Jalte Kabhi Bujhte Chirag', 'Kuch Ankahe Ehsas', 'Prkriti Ki Gungunahat','Ujale Tumhare Hain', 'Chhappan Pushpmalaen Kanha Ko Arpit', ' Shaym Ka He Dhyan Kar', 'Jeevan Ka Aadhar Tum', 'Bhajo Madhav, Bhajo Keshav', ' Bahut Priy Naam Govinda' "Kanha Ke Hm Sb Aabhari" & "Sharan Aaye Tumhari Hum" and one collection of stories entitled 'Aadmi Bne Rehne Ka Dhong'.

Her literary journey continues with a great endeavour. She has gone through many ups and downs in her life that have directed her vision towards suffering and she expresses that with her pen. Her writings reflect her closeness to nature, life, spirituality and humanity. For her, poetry is a God-gifted boon, and she wishes to fly high wearing the wings of poetry. She has contributed to more than 100 national and international English anthologies so far. She is a regular contributor to various national and international magazines, newspapers and journals. She has translated many poems by other poets into English, Hindi and Punjabi languages. She runs a blog about the Punjabi translations of English poems by different poets throughout the world. She is the chief-editor of two online e-zines, ***"CANVAS OF THOUGHTS" & "BHAV GAGAR"*** *in English and Hindi languages respectively. Her first poetry book in the Punjabi will be published shortly. She is an active member of various literary and creative platforms and has won several awards in writing competitions organised by these platforms. She won a 'gold and silver medal' in a Poetic World Cup contest held by Nigeria in February and May 2018 respectively, the 'Prasanna Jenn Memorial Award 2018' by the Asian Literary Society, and '5th place in the international essay writing competition on skin complexion discrimination' organised by the Literary Society of India in March 2018. One of her essays, 'Our role and responsibilities towards nation', was selected in a national essay writing competition and is part of the book 'Youth as Nation Builders.*

She is a famous name in Hindi literature, too. She writes poems, songs, ghazals, stories, essays, letters, articles and vivid forms of Hindi compositions. Besides her seven independent Hindi books, her Hindi writings are part of several international and national anthologies, newspapers, journals and magazines. She has won many awards for her Hindi writings. Her many projects are underway.

Besides poetry, she is also fond of painting, singing, cooking, knitting, designing, stitching, embroidery teaching and reading, She has won many awards in art competitions. Many of her paintings have been placed on the cover pages of various magazines. Even she herself designed the cover pages of her two English solo books entitled "Fountain of Inspirations" and "Canvas of Life...With My Pen". She is actively contributing to literature via her literary YouTube channel, Facebook page, blog, and Instagram page.

Born and brought up in a family of well-educated people, Dr. Sonia is living her life with simplicity and a mission to do something meaningful. She considers her family her biggest inspiration, as they have always motivated her in each and every phase of her life. She feels proud to have such grandparents who have enriched their children and grandchildren with ideal virtues and morals. Her grandfather is retired from the Indian Army and serves selflessly for society till today, even at the age of 97, and believes in doing his tasks on his own. Her grandmother left this materialistic world in 2020. She was a homemaker, who not only taught her Hindi language since her birth but also made her capable of learning other skills like cooking, knitting and embroidery. Dr. Sonia lost her father, Late Sh. Devinder Kumar, in April 2019, who retired as a Government English Lecturer. He lived his entire life for his children's bright future, and it is his efforts that have led Dr. Sonia and her brothers achieve their goals. As a teacher, he was a renowned name in academics who guided a number of students who are working in well-recognized positions in society today. She is living her life following his teachings and footprints. Her mother, Mrs. Nirmal Devi, is retired as a private secretary from the Higher Education Department. Panchkula, Haryana. She is her best friend, who has always motivated and accompanied her in her every adventure, whether related to her profession, passion or personal life. Dr. Sonia feels fortunate to get two younger brothers, who have always stood beside her in even the darkest phases of her life, encouraging her to move ahead. She considers them the pillars of her life. One of her brothers works as a project manager at USA based company in Houston, Texas, USA. and the youngest one is acting as a manager in the MARTUI company, Manesar, Gurugram, Haryana. He is a professional singer and is training his 9-year-old son in classical music. She feels happy to have her bhabhi like her younger sister, who has always been her best companion. She feels blessed to have many teachers who not only taught her professional skills but also appreciated her passionate ventures and today they also clap for her achievements. As a person, she is a less talkative, simple, humble, hard-working and determined personality. She prefers to utilise every single moment in doing something meaningful rather than wasting it in gossiping. She loves to work in a disciplined and organised way. She has completed her many poetry books while travelling to her work place. She is a deep believer in God and a great devotee of Lord Krishna. She is a member of the 'Mahila Mandal Sangeet Samiti' of many temples in her region and frequently participates in various religious events where she sings religious songs composed with her own pen. Her many religious books are in the process of publication.

Dr. Sonia Gupta is a renowned name in her professional field, too. She is working as an Associate Professor in the Oral Pathology Department at a Dental College near her home town. Recently, she has earned a fellowship in Forensic Odontology under Indian Board of Forensic Odontology. She serves the community by providing dental care. She has several scientific publications in PubMed and Scopus-indexed national and international journals with first authorship, and many more are under review. She is also working on three textbooks of dentistry. She is acting as a reviewer of various medical and dental journals. She actively takes part in various conferences, workshops, community health programmes and events and has presented several research papers and posters. She is a dedicated academician with the goal of making her students excel in their subjects and in developing their multitalented skills. She is enjoying her professional as well as literary journey, which is full of passion and mission.

- ***ADDRESS-*** *#95/3, Adarsh Nagar, Dera Bassi, Dist: Mohali, Punjab-140507, India.*
- ***MOBILE-*** *6280420736*
- ***FACEBOOK ID*** *- 100004964983747@facebook.com*
- ***FACEBOOK PAGE*** *- https://www.facebook.com/sonia4840/*
- ***BLOG*** *- http://drsoniablogspot.blogspot.in/*
- ***PUNJABI TRANSLATION BLOG*** *- http://passionatepunjabijourney.blogspot.com/*
- ***E MAIL*** *-drsoniagupta82@gmail.com.*

ANTHOLOGIES COMPLIED & EDITED BY DR. SONIA GUPTA TILL DATE

1. Words Cannot Define Her
2. Known Yet Unknown
3. Melodious Musings of Love
4. Me and My Valentine
5. Listen to Her Silence
6. Save Our Paradise
7. Whole World in a Single Word
8. Goddess on the Earth
9. Guiding Light on Our Earthly Path
10. You Cannot Be Replaced
11. Hues of Friendship
12. Bonding Beyond World
13. Verses of Patriotism
14. Glory of Indian Independence
15. Invisible Yet Everywhere
16. Above Us All
17. Awakener of Hidden Potentials
18. Amazing Gardener
19. Epitome of Innocence
20. Blooming Flowers in the Garden of Life
21. Life: Untying the Knot
22. Life: A Journey to Adore
23. A Voyage Through Memories
24. Flashback of the Past
25. Doorways to the New Beginnings
26. Me and My Magic Wand
27. Vivid Colours of Passion
28. Miracles of Determination
29. Music: The Elixir of Life
30. Smile: A Magical Magnetic Pull
31. Be thankful to Become Blissful
32. Gratitude- An Amazing Catalyst for Joy

LIST OF POETS

FAITH:
SILENT STRENGTH

(An Anthology Of Poems)

(Paperback, 1st Edition, NOVEMBER 2024)

Compiled & Edited By
Dr. Sonia Gupta

1. Faith: Silent Strength

O' dear, why afraid of gloom of darkness?
A ray of hope always shines beyond hopelessness,
Unfold the curtain of despair and see the magic,
Beyond the world of darkness; there enchants a melodious music.

What happened if life today is surrounded by dark clouds?
One day it will glitter and you will smile aloud,
What if today you are floating in ocean of gloom?
Life full of joy is waiting beyond mournful doom!

May be today; all around a darkness of failure,
But day isn't away when successful crown you will wear,
O' loss and gain are two wheels of this life,
We have to embrace darkness; if wish to happily survive.

O' this life is an exam, you have to cross it,
Give your best, do not waste it,
Have FAITH in your potential in every adverse situation,
FAITH is the SILENT STRENGTH to fight as a weapon.

© Dr. Sonia Gupta
(Editor)
******Title Poem******

2. Wherever Life Takes

Wherever this life takes you, accept it happily,
Every moment the divinity flows, feel it deeply,
There are few obstacles in life, overcome them,
But life always moves dauntlessly.

We often look forward to a bright future,
In its hope, we ignore what the present offers,
Try to seek the happiness in small gifts of God,
He has blessed us with so many treasures.

Joys and sorrows are the two sides of life
These are the wheels on which our lives,
Who knows when death knocks at its door,
Keep smiling even amidst strife.

Life is beautiful, accept its every way,
Whether it brings a gloomy night or a bright day,
Live it, love it, adore it,
Have faith in yourself each and every day.

© Abhishek Gupta

About the Poet

Abhishek Gupta

(Gurugram, Haryana, India)

abhi.4870@gmail.com

He is not a regular poet but writes with passion in his leisure time. He writes in English, Hindi & Punjabi languages. He is also fond of music, singing, art and playing badminton, cricket and chess. Holding a degree in B-Tech (Electronics), he is working as a manager in Maruti Suzuki company at Manesar. He is also a professional singer, with his own YouTube channel. He actively participates in various creative and literary events and has received numerous awards for his skills and talents.

3. The Hub Called Faith

No one lacks faith that the stars are the night's goldmines,
Although while the Sun during the day shines,
The stars are on the unseen side lines,
No one lacks faith that day follows night,
And every dark chapter ensues with the bright.

Such faith is a blossom of irrepressible optimism and happiness,
With its stem nourished by earnest keenness and endurance,
And the fragrance it emanates perpetuates positive assurance.

Carry the torch of faith through your life's flow,
Carry its offshoot Hope to make you glow,
Hope's flower of overwhelming cheerfulness,
Interwoven with faith's fruitfulness,
Sculpts your destiny of energizing effulgence,
And blessed blissfulness.

About the Poet

Ambika Gibikote Tadipatri

(Sydney, Australia)

ambikaprasaddoo@gmail.com

She is a poet, playwright & writer. She writes in the English language. She is associated with various literary and creative platforms. Her work has been featured in several national and international magazines, journals, newspapers and anthologies. She has received many awards for her write-ups. She is also passionate about classical dancing, drama and scriptural studies. Holding multiple degrees and certificates, currently she is working as an English educator.

4. I Still Have Faith

I'm dragging my tired body along the wet sidewalk,
Unnecessary rain is in my face,
And I see a dreary day in the puddles,
Sluggish.

I'll come home and set everything,
Joy decided to play hide and seek with me,
And the day is hard,
Lay on my shoulder.

Do I want more? No, I guess,
Air with a tired sigh,
Breathes in monotonous November,
This autumn evening.

But still I have faith,
Spring will definitely come,
And I am sure,
My faith is strong.

About the Poet

Ana May

(Kazan, Republic of Tatarstan, Russia)

anamay05@mail.ru

She is a bilingual poet & writer. She writes in English & Russian languages. She is associated with various literary and creative platforms. She has authored 4 solo books. Her work has been featured in several national and international magazines, journals, newspapers and anthologies. She has received many awards for her write-ups. She is a graduated from Tomsk State University with a degree in Entrepreneurship and from Creative Writing School in the field of "Verlibr". Currently, she works as a freelance writer and an Entrepreneur.

5. My Companion

Amidst my life's struggle
Odds and strives
Nobody was there
Along with me.

Path was tough
Way was rough
Nobody to guide
I was wandering all alone.

Still, I was never alone
My self-belief
Was my solo
Forever companion.

© Anna Ferriero

About the Poet

Anna Ferriero

(Torre del Greco, Italy)

annaferriero71@yahoo.it

She is a bilingual poet, writer & translator. She writes in English & Italian languages. She is associated with various literary and creative platforms. Her work has been featured in several national and international magazines, journals, newspapers and anthologies. She has received many awards for her write-ups. She has translated many poems throughout the world into Italian language. She is a representative of Italy in India at Güncel Sanat Dergisi. Currently, she is a student, university researcher and doctor of honoris causa.

6. I Just Remember

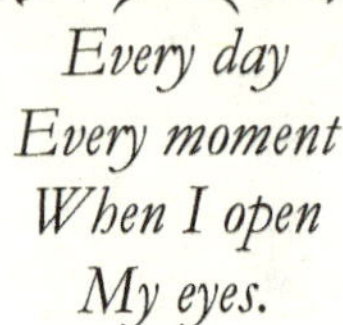

Every day
Every moment
When I open
My eyes.

I forget
All my pains
And worries
And miseries.

I just remember
My blessings
My achievements
My strengths.

Because…
I have firm faith
In my Almighty
He will always do good for me.

© ***Dr. Annie Evangelin.*** **N**

About the Poet

Dr. Annie Evangelin. N

(Vellore, Tamilnadu, India)

ann18eva@gmail.com

She is not a regular writer but writes with passion in her leisure time. She has contributed to many literary activities during her academic and professional career. By profession, she is a Dentist with a major specialty in Oral and Maxillofacial Surgery. She has received many accolades in her academics and profession.

❧❧❧

7. Faith Is a Tree

Expose your heart to the sun,
Let the monsoon come with rain,
Cultivate the small piece of heart,
With the plough of patience.

Get your heart fertilized then,
Sow the seeds of faith,
Water the plant again and again,
Access to light and air of depth.

Afforestation of faith with a campaign,
First time in the first attempt no gain,
May be hardship to bear the pain,
Lose not your confidence soon and mourn.

Keep on planting the tree of faith,
Inside the beautiful Garden of Heart,
Never dream the defeat in death,
The fruits of humanity never fall apart.

© Ayushi Pradhani

About the Poet

Ayushi Pradhani

(Balangir, Odisha, India)

pradhaniramesh212@gmail.com

She is a 14-year-old budding poet studying in 9th grade. She writes in the English language. She is also fond of reading, art, dancing and singing. She actively participates in various creative events organized by her school She has received many prizes for her creativity. She wishes to fly high spreading the wings of poetry.

8. Love Needs Faith

Love seeks no explanation,
It needs action.

Love doesn't speak,
But understands beyond doubt.

Love doesn't compare,
It shows care.

It needs the nutrients of faith to grow,
A wonderful impact it will throw.

Tie a bonding of love with faith,
No despair you will ever face.

About the Poet

Ayushman Pradhani

(Balangir, Odisha, India)

pradhaniramesh212@gmail.com

He is an 11-year-old budding poet studying in 8th grade. He writes in the English language. He is also fond of reading, art and music. He actively participates in various creative events organized by his school and other organizations. He has received many prizes for his creativity. He wishes to fly high spreading the wings of poetry.

9. Fatherly Earth

Immense development from Big Bang,
Many species came and lost,
But modern humans spotted,
Intelligent among all, but they struggled for survival.

Earth had enough for all,
Not for humans but for all organisms,
But earthly father worried for faithless human son,
Would his son occupy other's territories including father's?

Everywhere disturbance now,
Kingly trees are uprooted for development,
Singing birds are homeless now
Whom does the father share his grievance with now?

Fighting among monkeys for food,
Buildings are broken for skyscrapers,
Brothers are fighting for hereditary land,
Is there a word called 'faith' still existing in the world?

About the Poet

Damodar Boruah

(Kakodonga, Assam, India)

damodarboruah14@gmail.com

He is a bilingual poet, writer, author & translator. He writes in Assamese & English languages. He is associated with various literary and creative platforms. His work has been featured in several national and international magazines, journals, newspapers and anthologies. He has received many awards for his write-ups. Holding multiple degrees, currently, he is working as a farmer and Coacher for aspiring students to appear Sainik School and Jawahar Navodaya Vidyalaya Entrance Examinations.

10. Why?

We are taught
There is God in our life
If HE is present
Why are there conflicts?

Why there are
Tragedy destroying innocent life
We believe, then also
Why we are faced with problems?

We thought
God is full of Love
Then why there is no
Love In life?

As I reflect HE wants us
To believe
In believing we know there
Is a reason to believe.

About the Poet

David Soh

(Singapore)

davidsoh.books@gmail.com

He is a poet, writer & author. He writes in the English language. He has authored two independent poetry books. He is associated with various literary and creative platforms. His work has been featured in several national and international magazines, journals, newspapers and anthologies. He has received many awards for his write-ups. He is a high school graduate and currently working as a Financial Adviser Representative.

11. Our Belief in God

Since we are born and without any will of ours,
We learn from our societies to believe in what they believe,
Our minds are unable to know what the hidden truth is,
We learn in the dark caves of our society's beliefs.

But does a person believe in God, out of fear of Him,
Or pray to Him for a personal purpose?
And does he obey God out of fear,
Of His punishment and going to hell?

Is it enough for us to believe in the Almighty,
And do all the evil He has forbidden us?
For the sake of our evil selfish interests,
Should we claim to believe in Him?

© *Fady Bouaz*

About the Poet

Fady Bouaz

(Lebanon, Arab)

boazfady@gmail.com

He is a bilingual poet & writer. He writes in English & Arabian languages. He is associated with various literary and creative platforms. His work has been featured in several national and international magazines, journals, newspapers and anthologies. He has received many awards for his write-ups. Currently, he works as a carpenter and freelance writer.

12. I Waited Eagerly

I waited for him,
For I have full faith,
Since I have known him for decades-long,
Who studies about the universe,
And wants to leave a legacy,
Today I find him disordered.

Yes, still I patiently wait for him,
Silent he, mobile is off,
Nor I will call, but I know,
When will he leave me a message,
That will immortalize him for his behaviour,
His lines will scripted in golden words,
That will transform everyone's hearts.

© Glory Shikha Boruah

About the Poet

Glory Shikha Boruah

(Kakodonga, Assam, India)

damodarboruah14@gmail.com

She is a 17-year-old budding poet studying in 11th grade. She writes in the English language. She is also fond of reading, painting, dancing and singing. She actively participates in various creative events organized by her school She has received many prizes for her creativity. She got the inspiration of writing from his own father "Damodar Boruah" who is a poet. She wishes to fly high spreading the wings of poetry.

13. Feed Your Faith

What is real and abiding that justifies your heart?
It's when you give your best in the activities you start,
Faith is when you praise God in the stormy rain,
It's when you lift yourself from the anguish and pain.

It's when you trust Him in the valleys being dark,
You are resolute and feel hopeful when things are stark,
You praise God for He just cannot blatantly lie,
He will stand by you when you want to cry.

You'll succeed if you feed faith and starve your fear,
The evidence is that He wipes away every tear,
Faith is when you believe in Him in a failing marriage,
You believe in Him when you want a baby in a carriage.

Faith is when you don't know which direction to turn,
When you know He will heal every injury and burn,
Who had faith when everyone was at Church praying for rain?
The boy with an umbrella unhesitatingly, his prayers not in vain.

© Heera Nawaz

About the Poet

Heera Nawaz

(Bengaluru, Karnataka, India)

nawazheera@gmail.com

She is a poet & writer. She writes in the English language. She is associated with various literary and creative platforms. Her work has been featured in several national and international magazines, journals, newspapers and anthologies. She has received many awards for her write-ups. Holding an M.A. (English), currently, she is working as an educator and freelance writer.

14. My Indomitable Faith

It's what I cherish, within my heart,
That none can shake, or tear apart,
Believing all my future plans,
Will not end up in earth's dustpans.

Possessing strong faith, that's indestructible,
I cling to things, I deem incorruptible,
It is pure bliss, this faith, possessing,
I delight to share it, it's such a blessing.

When I look around, and see much sadness,
It gives me joy, to share my gladness,
A faith, I've learned to be dependable,
And consider it worthy, and indispensable.

I have faith, that when I look back on it,
I'll not mourn, being glad I kept track of it,
Holding my head up, basking in its ambiance,
With its lastingness, and absent transience.

About the Poet

Kathy Jo Blake-Bryant

(Bates City, Missouri, USA)

kathyjopoetree@gmail.com

She is a poet, writer & author. She writes in the English language. She has authored four independent poetry books. She is associated with various literary and creative platforms. Her work has been featured in several national and international magazines, journals, newspapers and anthologies. She has received many awards for her write-ups. She is a high school graduate and currently, working as a Domestic Engineer and enjoying her passion of poetry.

15. A Woven Tapestry

In the enormous sea of doubt
When shadows gather and the path is unclear
Faith is the compass that draws me near
To my ambition, that I crave
Guiding my troubled hearts
Through joy and through pain
In each broken moment
It weaves a thread for
A bright colourful tapestry
Which I could look back on.

© *Kavya Jha*

About the Poet

Kavya Jha

(Purnea, Bihar, India)

ashutoshjhapur@gmail.com

She is a 14-year-old budding poet studying in 10th grade. She writes in the English language. She is also fond of reading and music. She actively participates in various literary and creative events organized by her school and other organizations. She has received many prizes for her creativity. She wishes to fly high spreading the wings of poetry.

16. Miraculous Power

Sometimes I think
Sitting all alone
In my solitude.

What is that
Miraculous power
Which kept me survived
Even amidst my odds?

What was that power
That kept me smiling
Even amidst
My pains.

I realize at that moment,
That power is nothing
But my faith
In my Lord and myself.

© *Lynsey McCabe*

About the Poet

Lynsey McCabe

(Rhondda, South Wales, UK)

donna_salisbury@sky.com

She is a 14-year-old budding poet studying in the second year of comprehensive school. She writes in the English language. She is also fond of reading, art and music. She actively participates in various literary and creative events organized by her school and other organizations. She has received many prizes for her artwork and poetry. She got the inspiration for writing from her own mother, 'Donna McCabe'. She wishes to touch the heights of poetry.

17. His Determination

A bird
Flies high
Spreading his wings.

In search of
Food grains
For his children.

He has a fear
Of getting his wings
Cut by the world.

Yet, he never stops flying
Because he has a faith
In his determination.

About the Poet

Manhoman Rohilla

(Gurugram, Haryana, India)

rohillasahab9050@gmail.com

He is a 21-year-old budding poet studying in his final year, at Government Polytechnic. He is passionate about poetry and music. He writes in English & Hindi languages. He actively participates in various literary and creative events organized by his institute and other organizations. He has received many awards for his creativity. He wishes to go for a mile in the field of literature.

18. Oh Divine Lord

I wish to be submerged
Into the ocean of infinity
To feel complete
And realise my unfulfilled dreams
With the feeling of contentment
I believe in you like a blind - man
Putting trust and faith in you
Oh divine lord !
Give me the power
To decipher the difference
Between wrong and right.

About the Poet

Meemansa Jha

(Purnea, Bihar, India)

ashutoshjhapur@gmail.com

She is an 11-year-old budding poet studying in 8th grade. She writes in the English language. She is also fond of reading and music. She actively participates in various literary and creative events organized by her school and other organizations. She has received many prizes for her creativity. She wishes to fly high spreading the wings of poetry.

19. Strongest Weapon

Whatever may be
The situation
Whatever may be
The phase…

I will never lose
My determination
My self-belief
My confidence…

Afterall
Self-belief
Is the strongest weapon
To fight with any toughest situation.

About the Poet

Meena Panchal

(Faridabad, Haryana, India)

meenapanchl224@gmail.com

She is a 20-year-old budding poet studying in final year at Government Polytechnic, Faridabad. She is passionate about poetry and fashion designing. She writes in English & Hindi languages. She actively participates in various literary and creative events organized by her institute and other organizations. She has received many awards for her creativity. She wishes to go a mile in the field of literature along with her passion for fashion designing and art.

20. Why To Fear?

One day…
I asked the spider

O' dear spider
You knit your web
Falling again and again
Don't you have a fear
Of failure?

She smiled and replied
No dear
Why to fear
When my self-belief
Is with me…

About the Poet

Meher Mathur

(Pune, Maharashtra, India)

kshtjpandey879@gmail.com

She is a 6-year-old budding poet studying in 1st grade. She writes in the English & Hindi languages. She is also fond of drawing. She actively participates in various literary and creative events organized by her school and other organizations. She has received many prizes for her creativity. She wishes to fly high spreading the wings of poetry.

21. In Their Destiny

Rose stays
Along with thorns
Lotus blooms
Even amidst ponds.

Autumn remains bare
Embracing its torn leaves
Petals and bunches
Faded colours.

Yet all of these
Keep smiling
Having a faith
In their destiny.

© Muskan Vashisth

About the Poet

Muskan Vashisth

(Faridabad, Haryana, India)

muskanvashisht184@gmail.com

She is a 20-year-old budding poet studying in her final year at Government Polytechnic, Faridabad. She writes in English & Hindi languages. She is passionate about fashion designing and music. She actively participates in various literary and creative events organized by her institute and other organizations. She has received many awards for her creativity.

22. Blind Trust

I trusted on you
Blindly
More than
Anyone else
Even
Than myself
That you will
Never
Break up
My trust
My faith…

But
In the end
You did the same
And left me ashamed
Forever…

That's why
It is said
That
Don't trust anyone
Blindly…

© Namrata Dubey

About the Poet

Namrata Dubey

(Faridabad, Haryana, India)

nd7578509@gmail.com

She is a 23-year-old budding poet studying in her final year, data basement management. She is passionate about poetry and reading books. She writes in English & Hindi languages. She actively participates in various literary and creative events organized by her institute and other organizations. She has received many awards for her creativity. She wishes to spread positivity through her poetry.

23. Without Any Fear

My pen writes
On a blank paper
Boldly
Without any fear…

As it has
Firm faith
In its ink
And letters…

Whatever it will
Write
Will be for
Goodness of others.

About the Poet

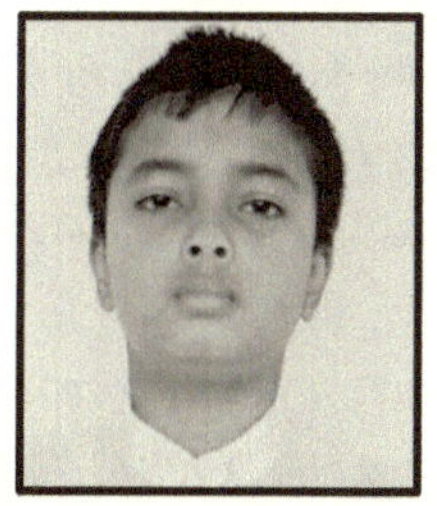

Nibir Neerlov Borah

(Titabor, Assam, India)
damodarboruah14@gmail.com

He is a 12-year-old budding poet studying in 6th grade. He writes in the English language. He is also fond of playing guitar. He actively participates in various literary and creative events organized by his school and other organizations. He has received many prizes for his creativity. He wishes to fly high spreading the wings of poetry.

24. Why There Is Hurry?

It takes some time for everything to happen in life,
Learn to have patience and faith,
Why there is hurry and worry, O' dear?

I know, you are in haste to reach the mission,
But it takes time to achieve that destination,
Why there is hurry and worry, O' dear?

I know, you have seen many dreams in your eyes,
But it takes time to cherish their reality with pride,
Why there is hurry and worry, O' dear?

I agree, time never waits for anyone,
But you have to wait for it to come,
Why there is hurry and worry, O' dear?

About the Poet

Nirmal Devi
(Mohali, Punjab, India)
nirmaldevi@gmail.com

She is not a regular poet but writes with passion. She writes in English, Hindi and Punjabi languages. She is also fond of art, singing, cooking, dancing and knitting. Retired as a personal secretary from Haryana Education Dept. Panchkula, currently, she works as a housewife and social worker.

25. We Cannot Understand

Faith!
O' faith!
From where do you come?
To where do you go?
Your mystery
Nobody of us knows.

You are so tender
And delicate
If broken
You tear the soul and heart
Deeply
We can't understand you fully.

About the Poet

Nishant Gupta

(Gurugram, Haryana, India)

abhi.4870@gmail.com

He is a 10 -year-old budding poet studying in 6th grade. He is passionate about poetry, music and art. He writes in English & Hindi languages. He is also a singer and getting training in classical music. He is fond of swimming, skating, playing badminton, cricket and chess. He actively participates in various literary and creative events organized by his school and other organizations. He has received many awards for his creativity. Recently, he performed as a singer in one of the renowned entertainment shows 'Junior Superstar Season-3' on Sony TV. He wishes to fly high spreading the wings of poetry and music.

26. Divinity

A child
Stays fearlessly
In a mother's womb
For nine months.

He has no fear
Of getting nutrition
Energy or
Anything else.

He just keeps
His faith
In the divinity of
His mother's love.

© Nishu Kushavaha

About the Poet

Nishu Kushavaha

(Faridabad, Haryana, India)

nishukmri2006@gmail.com

She is an 18-year-old budding poet studying in her 2nd year at Government Polytechnic, Faridabad. She is passionate about poetry and fashion designing. She writes in English & Hindi languages. She actively participates in various literary and creative events organized by her institute and other organizations. She has received many awards for her creativity. She wishes to bring a positive change in the world through her pen and art.

27. I Do Know

You love me endlessly
That I do know
For your spontaneous love
My head I bow.

You are my heart's queen
All the world knows
To see your loving heart
My hope here rose.

You are my dreams
And you are my heart
I have full faith in our love
None can take us apart.

© Dr. Okram Shakuntala

About the Poet

Dr. Okram Shakuntala

(Imphal, Manipur, India)

shakuntala.okram@gmail.com

She is a poet & writer. She writes in the English language. She is associated with various literary and creative platforms. Her work has been featured in several national and international magazines, journals, newspapers and anthologies. She has received many awards for her write-ups. Holding a Master in Arts and PhD, currently she works as an Asst. Prof of Economics and HOD, in The Maharaja Bodh Chandra College, Imphal.

28. Dauntless

My pain is not big for my love,
My poverty is not big for my dream,
My sorrow is not big for my anger,
My agony is not big for my revolt.

Noting is agreeable for me here,
Nothing is infallible for me here,
Bewitches me here no so-called purity,
Besieges me here no blare of bias.

Bleeding my heart is - a blast furnace,
Blazes it bad this blemishing society,
Blench I never and blast all blots,
Black my ink draws bright a tomorrow.

My self-belief is my greatest strength,
That will lead me to always win,
Even amidst my odds, I will stay strong,
Because my faith is strong even if I am alone.

© Prasant Misra

About the Poet

Prasant Misra

(Kashinagar, Odisha, India)

prasantmisra87@gmail.com

He is a bilingual poet & writer. He writes in English & Odia languages. He has authored four Odia and one English poetic collection. He is associated with various literary and creative platforms. His work has been featured in several national and international magazines, journals, newspapers and anthologies. He has received many awards for his write-ups. Holding an M.A. (Odia language and literature), currently, he is working as a journalist.

29. My Parents

In the entire world
If there is
Anyone
On whom
I trust
Are none
Other than
My parents…

I wish
To be their
Daughter
Always
Today
Tomorrow
And forever
Even beyond this life.

About the Poet

Radhika Rohilla

(Gurugram, Haryana, India)

radhikarohilla9050@gmail.com

She is a 17-year-old budding poet studying in her 2nd year at government Polytechnic. She is passionate about poetry and fashion designing. She writes in English & Hindi languages. She actively participates in various literary and creative events organized by her institute and other organizations. She has received many awards for her creativity. She wishes to go a mile in the field of literature along with her passion for fashion designing and art.

30. I Bow My Head

O' God!
Your greatness
Your magnanimity
Your grace…

Your kindness
Your generosity
Your empathy
Your compassion…

All are far beyond
This materialistic world
I bow my head to you
Having faith in your every gesture.

© *Ramanivas Tiwari*

About the Poet

Ramanivas Tiwari

(Sitapur, Uttar Pradesh, India)

ramanivas40@gmail.com

He is a bilingual poet and writer. He writes mostly in Hindi and less frequently in the English language. He is associated with various literary and creative platforms. His work has been featured in several national and international magazines, journals, newspapers and anthologies. He has received many awards for his Hindi write-ups. This is his first English anthology. Holding an M.A. (Hindi), he retired as a teacher and currently, works as a freelance writer and a social worker.

31. Believe Oneself

Believing in oneself makes stronger and sharper
Once one believes he dares forever a rover
Nothing or nobody can hinder him from shivering
Believe in what you do and become clever.

Determined I am when I believe in myself
Feeling encouraged, dynamic to quest
It gives me the strength, and stamina to do my best
An inspirational power of love does not let me rest.

It is a path of empowerment to achievement
Saves and makes me stand out of my predicament
Offering ample space for nourishment
Target fulfills evaporating the snow of puzzles and harassment.

It envelopes in humanity and solidarity
I can think of beyond-the-limit and anxiety
A transformation from individuality to generality
Hovering in the azure of futuristic society.

© Ramesh Chandra Pradhani

About the Poet

Ramesh Chandra Pradhani

(Balangir, Odisha, India)

pradhaniramesh212@gmail.com

He is a trilingual poet & writer. He writes in English, Hindi & Odia languages. He has authored six solo books. He is associated with various literary and creative platforms. His work has been featured in several national and international magazines, journals, newspapers and anthologies. He has received many awards for his write-ups. Holding multiple degrees, currently, he is working as a Principal at P S Degree Mahavidyalaya Deogaon, Odisha.

32.Faith Has A Power

At every step of life
Have self-confidence and faith in your inner potential
You will cherish amazing miracles.

A farmer sows a seed
In his fields
With a faith to have good growth of crops.

After the dark gloomy night
There arises the sun
Bringing a new morning every day.

All relations, bonding, friendships,
Are based on
A small word known as 'faith'.

If faith is there, everything exists,
If faith is broken, everything gets destroyed,
Faith has a power.

© Remy Pandey

About the Poet

Remy Pandey

(Bengaluru, Karnataka, India)

kshtjpandey879@gmail.com

She is a bilingual poet & writer. She writes in Hindi & English languages. She is associated with various literary and creative platforms. Her Hindi work has been featured in several international and national magazines, journals, anthologies and newspapers. She has won many awards for her write-ups. This is her first English anthology. She has a B. A philosophy Honours. Currently, she works as homemaker and freelance writer.

34. Surrender

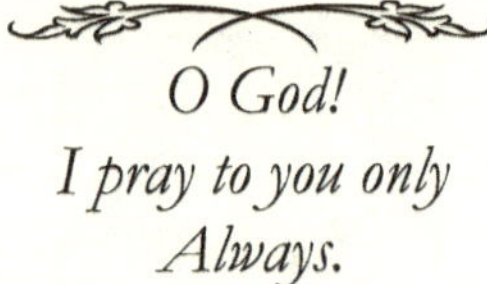

O God!
I pray to you only
Always.

I sing
Your glory
Always.

I don't need
Anyone else
Except you.

I have surrendered myself
To you
Believing in your greatness.

About the Poet

Rivyansh Rohilla
(Dehradun Uttarakhand, India
Rivyansh0312rohilla@gmail.com

Hi is a 12-year-old budding poet studying in 7 grade. He writes in the English language. He is also fond of reading, art and football playing. He actively participates in various creative events organized by his school and other organizations. He has received many prizes for his creativity. He wishes to fly high spreading the wing of poetry.

34. One Day

My little hands
Keep writing
On paper.

My little brain
Recalls all
Tables and rhymes.

I feel tough
And odd
Sometimes.

But then I keep
My faith
Strong.

That I will
Learn everything
One day.

About the Poet

Saanvi Gupta

(Gurugram, Haryana, India)

abhi.4870@gmail.com

She is a 7-year-old budding poet studying in 2nd class. She writes in English and Hindi languages. She is also fond of singing, playing badminton, skating and painting. She actively participates in various cultural events in her school and has received many prizes.

35. Actual Definition

To keep faith
Regardless of anything
Under any circumstances
Staying positive and
Trustworthy…

Is the actual
Definition of TRUST.

About the Poet

Sanchi Kumari

(Dera Bassi, Punjab, India)

Sunny128@gmail.com

She is a 6-year-old budding poet studying in 1st class. She writes in English and Hindi languages. She is also fond of singing, playing and painting. She actively participates in various cultural events in her school and has received many prizes.

❧❧❧

36. You are Always There

Life passes unnoticed
Rushes by in the blink of an eye
Only you are always there
I carry you in my heart.

I believe in you
And when my soul is failing
You lift me up then
You don't let me fall.

Dear God! forever
I believe in you
I believe in your love
I trust in your mercy.

When it's the hardest for me
You are here to show me the way
And give me strength
And power to fight.

About the Poet

Seadeta Bela Juric

(Bosnia and Herzegovina)

Seadetajurić@gmail. Com

She is a bilingual poet & writer. She writes in English & Bosnian languages. She is associated with various literary and creative platforms. Her work has been featured in several national and international magazines, journals, newspapers and anthologies. She has received many awards for her write-ups. Retired as a teacher, she is living as a housewife.

37. Broken

My faith was strong
None could break that
None could erase that
None could deny that.

But a flicker of doubt
Broken everything
Erased everything
Denied everything.

And left a question
Within my mind
Is it known as 'FAITH'?
Does it carry this much value?

Today my faith is broken
Leaving me all alone
I cannot trust now
On anyone.

About the Poet

Shalini Srivastava

(Lucknow, Uttar Pradesh, India)

shwetanshsri@gmail.com

She is a bilingual poet & writer. She writes in Hindi & English languages. She is associated with various literary and creative platforms. Her Hindi work has been featured in several international and national magazines, journals, anthologies and newspapers. She has won many awards for her write-ups. This is her first English anthology. Holding an M.A., B.Ed., and currently, she is working as a teacher.

38. His Existence

In every particle
Of this universe
There exists
Only God.

Even in the stones
And thorns
There is
The presence of Lord.

Entire world
Worships Him
Prays
Before Him.

It is the
Serene faith
In His existence
And omnipresence.

About the Poet

Shamsher Singh Rohilla

(Gurugram, Haryana, India)

shamshers44@gmail.com

He is a bilingual poet & writer. He writes in English & Hindi languages. He is associated with various literary and creative platforms. His work has been featured in several national and international magazines, journals, newspapers and anthologies. He has received many awards for his write-ups. Holding a B.A., currently he works as a Quality Officer in a private company.

39. I Think

People say
We trust you
We believe in you.

We know
You are with us
You will never betray us.

But I think
These wordings
Must be replaces.

They must say
We trust ourselves
We believe in ourselves.

We know
We are with ourselves
We will never betray ourselves.

About the Poet

Sheetal Kumari

(Faridabad, Haryana, India)

skumari06092007@gmail.com

She is a 17-year-old budding poet studying in her 2nd year of diploma in data base management at Government Polytechnic, Faridabad. She writes in English & Hindi languages. She is also passionate about fashion designing & music. She actively participates in various literary and creative events organized by her institute and other organizations. She has received many awards for her creativity.

40. What Tomorrow Brings

What tomorrow brings is a puzzle,
A mystery in the realm of the future,
If only we could solve the riddle,
Things would be so much easier.

Easier to chalk out a game plan ,
For intended events and more,
And execute it to perfection,
Chance to fail, we ignore.

Tomorrow can be a symbol of hope,
It's contents remaining concealed,
It will not afford the same scope
Should its essentials be revealed.

Tomorrow will bring what's writ in our fate,
A message of hope or news of sorrow,
With prayer on our lips and faith in our hearts,
Let us prepare ourselves to welcome tomorrow.

About the Poet

Dr. Shyamala Annavarapu

(Hyderabad, Telangana, India)

shyamala.annavarapu@gmail.com

She is a poet, writer & doctor. She writes in the English language. She is associated with various literary and creative platforms. Her work has been featured in several national and international magazines, journals, newspapers and anthologies. She has received many awards in academic as well as literature. She is a postgraduate in gynaecology and currently, working as a private practitioner.

41. Positive Thinker

If I am a positive thinker
I can view everything with
A special knack
Avoiding confusion and chaos
Pessimism hurts self-esteem and sometimes loses of confidence.

Age watches every minutest thing
Evaluates the scenario with utmost care
Faith catches the ideas of
oscillation and helps to manage things
tangible or visible.

It is immaterial...
If stands
In the labyrinth of problems,
A new energy
Is attained, as 'somebody' said...

About the Poet

Sreedharan Parokode

(Kozhikode, Kerala, India)

sreeparokode@gmail.com

He is a bilingual poet, writer, author & lyricist. He writes in English & Malayalam languages. He has 30 solo poetry books to his credit. He is associated with various literary and creative platforms. His work has been featured in several national and international magazines, journals, newspapers and anthologies. He has received many awards for his write-ups. Holding multiple degrees, he is retired from Calicut University. Currently, he is enjoying his literary journey.

❧❧❧

42. It's Possible

Even amidst
Heavy storms
Boats and sails
Keep sailing
Aiming to reach
At their
Destination…
It's all possible
Because of their
Self-belief
And determination.

Steven McCabe

About the Poet

Steven McCabe

(Rhondda, South Wales, UK)

donna_salisbury@sky.com

He is not a regular poet but writes with passion. He writes in the English language. He is also fond of music, traveling, playing football, going gym and having cars. He actively participates in various creative and literary events. He has served in the army for 4 years before leaving and getting married. Currently, he works full-time and takes care of his family.

43. Is It Your Faith?

I left
My home
My own world
Just For you...

I Forgot
My ambition
My dreams
Just For you...

I ignored
Every relation
Every bonding
Just For you...

Still, you doubt
On me...
Is it Your Faith..
In me?

About the Poet

Sudhir Meher

(Kalahandi, Odisha, India)

sudhirmeher69@gmail.com

He is a bilingual poet, writer & author He writes in Odia & English languages. He has authored 3 solo Odia poetry books. He is associated with various literary and creative platforms. His work has been featured in several national and international magazines, journals, newspapers and anthologies. He has received many awards for his write-ups. Holding M. Sc. & B. Ed. In chemistry, currently, he is working as a government teacher.

44. Connections

Lofty mountains, clouds gliding over
The river flows like a young girl's anklet
In search of the lover, the sea
The wind whispers, and the trees giggle
Flowers yearn for bees to sip their nectar
Lotus leaves aloof from water
The thread of trust binds everyone
Aura Grandeur of the world

The branches shelter the birds
For they trust in the tree
The vast ocean, teeming with life
Fishes, plants enjoy
Marriage unites two unknown souls
Sailing with belief and caressing each other
Family growing nurtured by love
The thread of trust binds everyone.

© *Sulochana Narayana*

About the Poet

Sulochana Narayanan

(Palakkad, Kerala, India)

sulsubra@gmail.com

She is a bilingual poet & writer She writes in English & Tamil languages. She has published a solo English poetry book "Imprints". She is associated with various literary and creative platforms. Her work has been featured in several national and international magazines, journals, newspapers and anthologies. She has received many awards for her write-ups. She is also fond of paintings, music and reading. Holding an M.A. (English) and B.Ed., currently, she works as an academician.

45. Safe Embrace

A little puppy
Was lying
So calm
Embracing his
Mother's arms
Even amidst
Hot scorching
Sunny day
With a faith
That his mother
Will save him
From all hurdles.

About the Poet

Sunny Kumae

(Dera Bassi, Punjab, India)

Sunny148@gmail.com

He is a 16 -year-old budding poet studying in 11th standard. He is passionate about poetry and music. He writes in English & Hindi languages. He actively participates in various literary and creative events organized by his institute and other organizations. He has received many awards for his creativity. He wishes to go for a mile in the field of literature.

46. In Faith

When adversity strikes in my sanguine life,
I feel crushing my heart and tearing my bones,
In the hardest situations of life, I boldly strive,
In tough, I stay grounded on my solid stones.

In the depth of adversity, I swim it across;
The invincible pride provides me strength above,
With patience, I gain victory, never in a loss,
In faith, I can fly higher like the peaceful dove.

My adversity becomes diamond dust with potent,
My perseverance overcomes, never let me down,
The hardest time leads me to my greatest moment,
Beyond adversity, there awaits my glittering crown.

About the Poet

Surendra Singnar

(Diphu, Assam, India)

Singnar.s@gmail.com

He is a bilingual poet & writer. He writes in English & Assamese languages. He has authored 2 solo poetry books. He is associated with various literary and creative platforms. His work has been featured in several national and international magazines, journals, newspapers and anthologies. He has received many awards for his write-ups. Retired as a high school teacher, currently, he works as a social worker.

47. A Spark Within

Belief, a spark within the soul,
That lifts the heart and makes it whole,
It sees beyond the veil of fear,
And whispers, "Truth is always near."

When doubt surrounds it, it holds its ground,
A quiet sound, a silent strength,
In every trial, every trial challenge,
Belief walks with us all the while.

No sign it needs, no proof it seeks,
Just trust in what the spirit feeds,
For in belief, the world unfolds,
A faith that shapes the dreams it holds.

Belief is the seed that dares to grow,
In barren lands where doubt may flow,
It trusts in paths yet unexplored,
And finds its wings without a sword.

© *Taghrid Bou Merhi*

About the Poet

Taghrid Bou Merhi

(Foz Do Iguaçu, Paraná, Brasil)

taghrid240@gmail.com

She is a multilingual poet, writer, editor, translator and journalist. She has authored 17 books and translated 24 books to date. She is associated with various literary and creative platforms. Her work has been featured in several national and international magazines, journals, newspapers and anthologies. She has received many awards for her write-ups. Currently, she is working as an Arabic language teacher for non-native speakers.

48. For Ages of Ages

Not loving you is a sin,
So I am virtuous,
In this pilgrimage, this is all,
I don't know its purity,
I don't understand the chant.
Leave the favourite poems and pick up the white pages,
If you want to cover everything, you can.

The light that touches you becomes a shadow,
What do you know why the outrage,
Run to summer paths,
At the end of the classes of thirsty birds,
I grab the chalk from the waiting hands,
I write with my chest full - I'm fine with virtue !
Not loving you is a sin,
I have been saying this for ages of ages.

© Tapas Mahapatra

About the Poet

Tapas Mahapatra

Kolkata, West Bengal, India,

tapasmahapatra025@gmail.com

He is a bilingual poet, writer, author & translator. He writes in Bengali & English languages. He has authored 8 solo Bengali Poetry books. He is associated with various literary and creative platforms. His work has been featured in several national and international magazines, journals, newspapers and anthologies. He has received many awards for his write-ups. He is a Graduate of Calcutta University and currently works as a journalist.

49. Together We

You there, let me share a word,
We float on the same surface,
You rise your head high and,
Look up with pomp and grace.

I'm hesitant, shaking from within,
Cause I've crawled a long way,
From caves, bars, and veneration,
A coloured form out of clay.

Give me a hand...
Lift me up...
Take me to your side...

I will shine with you, combine,
Soar to pierce through blues,
Together, we will earth design,
A rainbow of equal values.

About the Poet

Dr. Tejaswini Deepak Patil

(Karad, Maharashtra, India)

tejaswinipatil70@gmail.com

She is a trilingual poet, writer and editor. She writes in the English, Hindi & Marathi languages. She's authored 4 English and 1 Hindi solo books and edited 6 anthologies. She is associated with various literary and creative platforms. Her work has been featured in several national and international magazines, journals, newspapers and anthologies. She is Founder Director of INNSÆI Journal and MatruAkshar Journal. She has received many awards for her write-ups. Holding an M.A., M. Phil. & Ph.D. in English literature, currently, she is working as an Associate Professor in English at Arts and Commerce College, Kasegaon, Dist. Sangli, Maharashtra.

50. O' Life Listen

O' Life listen,
You may have millions of reasons,
To break us down,
To snatch our glorious crown.

You may bring hurdles on our way,
You may make tough our each day,
You may bring tears,
You may try to indulge fears.

Yet we will never be broken,
With determination, we will move on,
Keeping the flicker of self-belief always alive,
We will fearlessly and boldly survive.

We will prove you wrong,
We will sing joyful song,
Even amidst despair, we will keep smiling,
We will never lose our faith, you can do anything.

About the Poet

Vikas Gupta

(Mississauga, Ontario, Canada)

Vikas.48@gmail.com

He is not a regular poet but writes with passion. Holding degrees in B-Tech and MBA, he is working as a project manager in one of the multinational companies in the USA. He writes in English, Hindi and Punjabi languages. He is also fond of music, art, cooking, reading, traveling, and photography. He actively participates in various creative and literary events.

51. Belief Is a Must

The journey of life is built on faith and trust,
From beginning to end, belief is a must.

Whenever the boat of life gets stuck in a whirlpool,
Life becomes tough, uneasy, and uncool.

Only through effort do we build confidence,
And by that, we achieve our goal hence.

When we are unable to fight,
And there seems no ray of light.

Trust in yourself to show the way,
And all the odds will fade away.

About the Poet

Dr. Vinod Kumar Gupta

(Noida, Uttar Pradesh, India).

atalmoradabadi@gmail.com

He is a bilingual poet & writer. He writes in English & Hindi languages. He is associated with various literary and creative platforms. His work has been featured in several national and international magazines, journals, newspapers and anthologies. He has received many awards for his write-ups. His first solo Hindi book is coming soon. Holding multiple degrees, he retired as an Engineer and currently, works as a freelance writer & social worker.

FAITH

FAITH:
SILENT STRENGTH

(AN ANTHOLOGY OF POEMS)

(PAPERBACK, 1ST EDITION, NOVEMBER 2024)

COMPILED & EDITED BY
DR. SONIA GUPTA

FAITH

"Life is uncertain full of odds & struggles. Amidst these adverse phases, keep faith in your inner potential, every hurdle is crossed itself. Faith is the silent strength to keep us survive even in such tough situations."

DR. SONIA GUPTA

Keep the faith

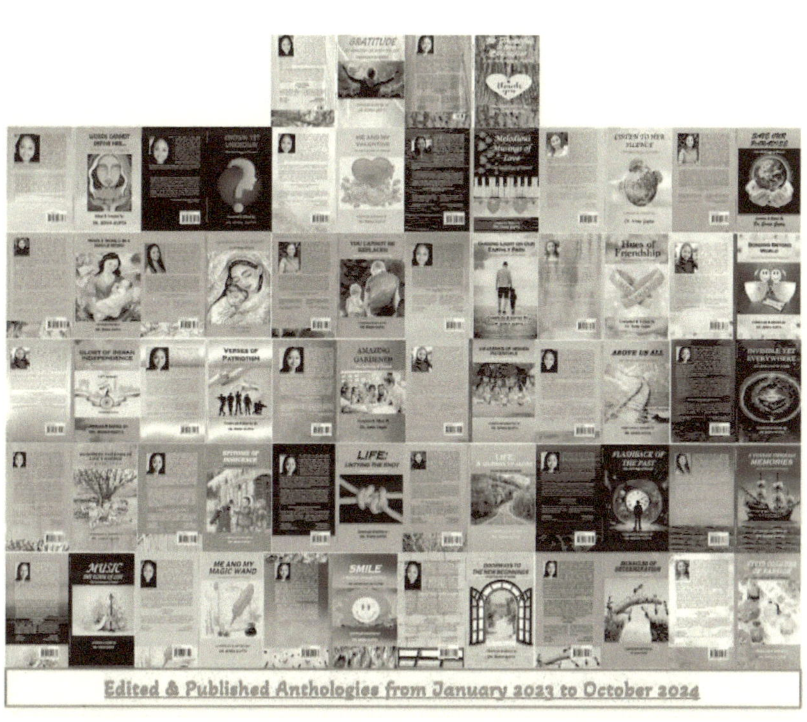

Edited & Published Anthologies from January 2023 to October 2024

www.ingramcontent.com/pod-product-compliance
Lightning Source LLC
LaVergne TN
LVHW091057150826
845673LV00002B/620

* 9 7 9 8 8 9 6 1 0 1 0 9 3 *